The
Statue
of Liberty

The Statue of Liberty

America's Proud Lady

Jim Haskins

Lerner Publications Company • Minneapolis

Manufactured in the United States of America

LIBRARY OF CONGRESS CATALOGING-IN-PUBLICATION DATA

Haskins, James, 1941-
  The Statue of Liberty, America's proud lady.

  Includes index.
  Summary: A history of America's most famous statue,
discussing how it was built and why it was given to the
United States.
  1. Statue of Liberty (New York, N.Y.) — Juvenile
literature. 2. Statue of Liberty National Monument
(New York, N.Y.) — Juvenile literature. 3. New York
(N.Y.) — Buildings, structures, etc. — Juvenile literature.
[1. Statue of Liberty (New York, N.Y.) 2. National
monuments] I. Title.
  F128.64.L6H37   1986   974.7'1   85-18061
  ISBN 0-8225-1706-X (lib. bdg.)

1 2 3 4 5 6 7 8 9 10 94 93 92 91 90 89 88 87 86

ACKNOWLEDGMENTS

I am grateful to Sheila McCauley, Director, National Student Campaign, The Statue of Liberty-Ellis Island Foundation, Inc., to J. Edward Easler, II, Director, Southeast Region, The Statue of Liberty-Ellis Island Foundation, Inc., to Ann Kalkhoff, and to Kathy Benson for their help.

Contents

Over 2 million tourists visit the Statue of Liberty every year.

What the Statue Means

1

We call her simply The Statue of Liberty. The lady with a torch in one hand and a tablet in the other is a symbol of freedom and equality, a symbol of America. Standing more than 300 feet above New York Harbor, she has watched thousands of immigrants arrive in America, first by steamship, now usually by airplane.

If you take the special ferryboat out to Liberty Island to see the Statue of Liberty, you will hear the other people on the boat speaking many different languages. As you walk up to her pedestal, you will see the famous words written by the poet Emma Lazarus:

> Give me your tired, your poor,
> Your huddled masses yearning to breathe free,
> The wretched refuse of your teeming shore.
> Send these, the homeless, tempest-tost to me,
> I lift my lamp beside the golden door!

And, if you are like most Americans, you will feel a great pride in your country, a nation of immigrants who managed to live together in spite of their differences and to work together to build a strong and free country.

It comes as a surprise to many Americans to learn that, officially at least, the Statue of Liberty did not always symbolize America's freedom. The statue's real name is Liberty Enlightening the World, and when funds were being raised in the United States for her pedestal, the only way the U.S. Congress would agree to spend any money was by considering the statue a lighthouse that would help ships entering the harbor. In fact, for many years the Lighthouse Bureau was responsible for the upkeep of the statue.

While the people of France raised the money for the actual statue, it was up to the people of the United States to raise the money for her base and pedestal. That took so long that the statue, which was supposed to mark the one hundredth anniversary of the end of the war of independence from England in 1883, was not dedicated until three years later, in 1886.

It seems hard to believe that Americans would be so reluctant to contribute to such a fine symbol. But then, it is also hard to believe how few people actually fought for America's freedom in the Revolutionary War and how poorly equipped and fed and paid they were. If the American colonists had really supported the men who were fighting for their independence, that horrible winter that General George Washington and his troops spent at Valley Forge, Pennsylvania, would not have happened.

Sometimes an idea arises before a lot of people are ready to accept it. Sometimes people with little power see the real meaning of an idea before the people who enjoy great power can understand it. That is what happened in the case of the Statue of Liberty. Emma Lazarus's poem was not inscribed on the statue's base until seventeen years after the statue was dedicated. The statue did not become a national monument until 1924. But the new Americans, the immigrants, had decided that the statue was a symbol of America's opportunity almost from the beginning. Today, nearly everyone shares that idea.

The people who believe that the Statue of Liberty is a symbol of opportunity for all now even include Americans who did not come as immigrants. The ancestors of most black Americans did not come to America because they were seeking greater opportunity. They were brought here against their will as slaves. They did not enter the United States through the immigration station at Ellis Island, near Liberty Island; instead, they came by way of the slave markets in New Orleans, Louisiana, Savannah, Georgia, and other places.

Slavery had been abolished in the United States when Liberty Enlightening the World was dedicated in New York Harbor in 1886, but blacks did not enjoy equal rights as citizens. Still, in the hundred years since the statue was dedicated, blacks have gained the same legal rights as other Americans. And it was the sons and daughters of the white immigrants who helped to ensure that blacks, too, would have an opportunity to share in the promise of America. Most people do not realize that one of the reasons the statue was given by the people of France to the people of the United States was to honor America for abolishing slavery (even though it took a Civil War to do it) and still preserving the Union. In the eyes of the French people, the United States was living up to the wonderful ideas of liberty set forth in the Declaration of Independence.

The Birth of the Statue of Liberty

2

"We hold these truths to be self-evident,
that all men are created equal, that they are endowed
by their Creator with certain unalienable Rights,
that among these are Life, Liberty and the pursuit
of Happiness."

These words from the Declaration of Independence had a strong effect on many French people who lived in a land dominated by priests and by the noble class and who did not enjoy either religious freedom or political equality. During the American Revolution, thousands of French troops had fought with the colonial rebels against England. A young French nobleman, the Marquis de Lafayette, had fought side by side with General George Washington. The Treaty of Versailles, which officially ended the war of the American Revolution, was signed by representatives from Great Britain and the United States at Versailles, France, in 1783.

After the colonies won their independence from Great Britain and formed the United States of America, many Frenchmen looked to the new country as a model of freedom. In 1789, French peasants revolted against their king, Louis XVI, but they did not succeed in creating a democratic country like the United States. America remained for them an ideal of liberty. And as the young country went through the pains of growing up, ordinary Frenchmen watched closely and cheered its attempts to live up to the ideas on which it had been founded.

To these ordinary French people, one of the most obvious failures of the United States to live up to its ideals was the institution of slavery. How could a country that believed that "all men are created equal" allow people to be slaves?

The question of slavery, among other problems, so divided the United States that in 1861 the South left the Union and the Civil War broke out. Over in France, the people in positions of power supported the Southern states. They made no secret of their hope that the Union would be destroyed and that democratic government would be proved a failure. They thought that President Abraham Lincoln was a comic character, a country bumpkin, and when he was assassinated by John Wilkes Booth they really didn't care.

But the ordinary French people cared, and so did ordinary people in other European countries. In fact, there was such an outpouring of sorrow over Abraham Lincoln's death that upper class Europeans were shocked. They had no idea that the common people saw Lincoln as a symbol of American liberty and as a hero who was trying to preserve democratic government by preserving the Union of the States.

In Paris, people mourned as if they had lost a friend. One of the city's newspapers came up with the idea of giving a gold medal to the slain president's widow, Mary Todd Lincoln, and people sent in money to pay for it. But the French emperor, Napoleon III, did not want the common people of Paris to make such a gesture. He had the money seized, along with the list of people who had donated it. But he could not stop the plan. Eventually a gold medal was sent to President Lincoln's widow, but it was done in secret. The medal was made in Switzerland, sneaked into France to the American ambassador, and then secretly taken to America in a diplomatic pouch. Here is the English translation of the inscription on the medal:

"Dedicated by French democracy to Lincoln, twice-elected President of the United States—honest Lincoln who abolished slavery, reestablished the union, and saved the Republic, without veiling the Statue of Liberty." (The term, "Statue of Liberty," did not, of course, refer to any real statue, but to an idea.)

Two men who had helped raise money for the medal and seen to it that it reached Mrs. Lincoln were Édouard de Laboulaye, a lawyer, teacher and writer, and Frédéric Auguste Bartholdi, a sculptor.

15

They probably also had something to do with the wording of the inscription on the medal, for they had already started to talk about raising money so they could give the people of the United States some sort of monument to liberty. There was no such thing as a "Statue of Liberty" in the United States or anywhere else. But if Laboulaye and Bartholdi had their way, there would be such a statue someday.

Frédéric Auguste Bartholdi was a master of monuments. His huge sculptures were in public squares in several French cities. He was excited not only about creating a monument to liberty but also about having one of his works in the United States. In 1871 he visited the United States for the first time and traveled all around the country, trying to understand America and what it was to be an American. The only clear conclusions he came to were that America was a vast and varied country and that his monument should be set in a huge, open space so that it would not look colossal except if one were right next to it. He had chosen as his site an island in New York harbor that had been owned by a wealthy Dutch merchant named Isaac Bedloo back in the 1600s. It was now called Bedloe's Island (over the years the spelling of the name had changed). The federal government had taken over the island in 1800 and built a star-shaped fort there.

Bartholdi first saw the island as his steamship

from France entered the harbor after a stormy thirteen-day voyage. It was early morning, and all around him his fellow passengers were cheering and offering thanks for the sight of land at last. He later wrote, "The picture that is presented to the view when one arrives at New York is marvelous; when, after some days of voyaging, in the pearly radiance of a beautiful morning is revealed the magnificent spectacle of those immense cities, of those rivers extending as far as the eye can reach, festooned with masts and flags; when one awakes, so to speak, in the midst of that interior sea covered with vessels, some giants in size, some dwarfs, which swarm about puffing, whistling, swinging the great arms of their uncovered walking beams, moving to and fro like a crowd upon a public square, it is thrilling. It is indeed the New World which appears in its majestic expanse, with the ardor of its glowing life." Right then and there, Bartholdi decided that New York Harbor would be the "public square" for his statue.

Back in France, he gave detailed reports of his travels to Édouard de Laboulaye, and the two talked about what the statue should look like and how much money would be needed to build it. At first, they spoke of having the statue finished and in place in time for the celebration of America's centennial, the one hundredth anniversary of the Declaration of Independence. But the organized campaign to raise the necessary funds to pay for the statue didn't even get started until 1875, the year before the centennial. In the meantime, both Laboulaye and Bartholdi had other work to attend to. Laboulaye was working to establish France as a Constitutional Republic. Even if he'd had the time to devote to a fundraising campaign, he realized that it was not a good time to ask his countrymen for money to build a monument in America. France was getting over a war with Prussia and had much rebuilding to do in its own cities.

Bartholdi was kept busy designing other monuments for the United States. One was a bronze statue of Lafayette, which the French government was presenting to New York on behalf of French residents there. Another was a cast-iron fountain, ordered by the city of Philadelphia for its one hundredth anniversary. Still another was a series of sculptures of Great Americans for a church in Boston. But all the while he kept working on sketches and models for the great monument to liberty.

He decided early on that the statue would be the figure of a woman in long flowing robes. In one hand held high, she would carry a torch, the torch of liberty. At first, he had the torch in her left hand; later, he changed it to the right hand. At first, she was a very defiant figure. Later, he made her more remote, removed from the everyday affairs of man. At first, she held a broken chain in her

Frédéric Bartholdi at work in his Paris studio beside a model of Lady Liberty.

19

Two early clay models of the Statue.

other hand, to symbolize the broken chains of bondage. Later, Bartholdi decided that she would hold a tablet and that on it would be inscribed the date July IV, MDCCLXXVI (July 4, 1776). The fragment of chain would be on the ground, as if she had already thrown it there. The statue's head wear also changed over the years, from a small crown to a simple drape to a large, spiked crown. One thing that did not change was the face, for which Bartholdi used his own mother as a model.

Since his mother was not strong enough to stand for hours while he modeled the statue's body, Bartholdi searched for a younger woman for that job. The young woman who posed for him, Jeanne-Emilie Baheux de Puysieux, eventually became his wife. Bartholdi made many sketches and plaster models, but he knew that he could not be sure exactly how the statue would look until he actually built it. It was to be so huge that he was bound to run into some problems that he could not foresee until he actually began. Also, he would be using a process he had never worked with before. He would not carve the statue in stone or cast it in bronze. Instead, he would construct a skeleton of wood, stone, and iron and hammer thin sheets of copper over it.

In Bartholdi's work-shop, the wooden skeleton of the Statue's left hand, and the plaster-covered full-size version. Note the half-size model of the hand and the fourth-size model of the head in the background of the lower photo.

The Lady Comes Alive

3

Using his own money, plus donations from friends and acquaintances, Bartholdi began work on his statue. Working in the largest studio he could find, with as many assistants as he could afford, he made a thirty-six foot plaster model of the statue, one-fourth the size of the finished work. Then, he divided the thirty-six foot model into about three hundred sections. Each section was then covered with dots to be used as guides in making a section for the finished model that would be exactly four times bigger. This was a very complicated process; about nine thousand measurements had to be made for each section. Any mistake would result in an error four times bigger on the finished statue.

The next step was to make a plaster mold for each section that was the size of that section on the finished statue. Then, carpenters made an exact copy of that section with wooden strips, a kind of latticework skeleton. After that, metalworkers pounded huge, thin sheets of copper over the lattice-work skeleton. When they had to do details or complicated shapes, they heated the copper first so it would be more malleable.

The stern face of Liberty was modeled after Bartholdi's mother. Here it awaits assembly with the rest of the head.

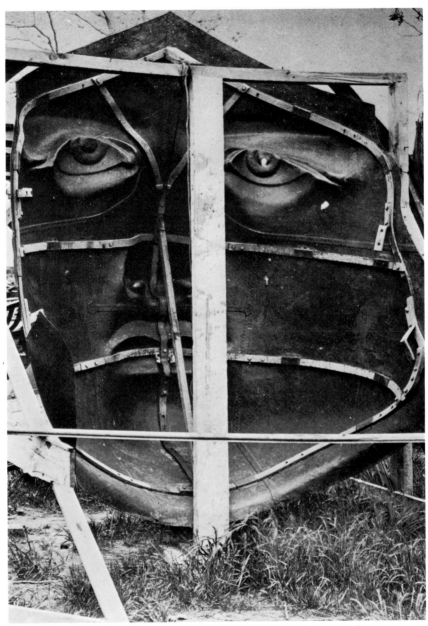

The iron framework and the seams which join the copper skin are visible behind the Statue's face.

Bartholdi chose to work on the arm and the torch first. He wanted something to be finished in time for the American centennial in 1876, and a full-scale model of the arm and torch did go on display in Philadelphia that year. From there, it went on to New York City, where it was displayed at Madison Square. Bartholdi and his French friends wanted Americans to pay for the pedestal on which the statue would stand, and Bartholdi hoped that seeing the arm and torch would encourage Americans to start raising the necessary funds. But while the sight of the huge model did excite some Americans, it caused others to become suspicious. A writer for the *New York Times* wanted to know why Bartholdi had started with the arm instead of the foot. He implied that maybe Bartholdi never intended to make the whole statue and was just trying to dupe Americans out of their money.

Bartholdi knew how to handle the New York resistance to his project. He started suggesting to his friends in Philadelphia that their city might be a better place for his statue. As soon as New Yorkers heard that, they changed their tune. The *New York Times* editors quickly decided that the statue belonged in New York Harbor, and anyway the light from the torch would be useful to ships entering the harbor at night.

On July 4, 1876, Bartholdi paid another visit to Bedloe's Island. He chose that date because he hoped it would bring good luck to his project. During that visit, he decided that his statue should face out toward the harbor, rather than toward the land. He made his decision after he watched a ship packed with immigrants steaming in from the Atlantic and thought how nice it would be for them to be welcomed by the torch of freedom. He also suggested at that time that the name of the island be changed to Liberty Island, but no one paid much attention to him.

When he returned to France, Bartholdi continued to work on the statue, and in July 1881 he announced that it would be ready in 1883, in time for the one-hundredth anniversary of the end of the Revolutionary War. But over in the United States very little money had been raised for the pedestal. In fact, not until May 1883 were any substantial funds raised. That's when Joseph Pulitzer, editor of the New York *World*, decided to take matters into his own hands. He launched a campaign to raise the necessary funds from the ordinary people of New York, since the millionaires couldn't seem to raise the money.

Pulitzer printed in the *World* the names of all the people who donated money. His campaign inspired artists and writers to help raise funds for the pedestal. A group of artists held a benefit exhibition, and some writers assembled a collection to go along with it. A poet named Emma Lazarus wrote a poem

Bartholdi's workmen began assembling the Statue in France in October 1881. By midsummer, 1882, Liberty's copper skin extended up to her waist. She was not finished until June, 1884, and did not make the trip to America until the next year.

After she was entirely assembled outside Bartholdi's Paris workshop, on a steel framework designed by Gustave Eiffel, Liberty was taken apart again. The pieces were numbered so that she could be completely rebuilt in New York.

titled "The New Colossus" for the collection. It was a wonderful poem, and it gave real meaning to the idea of the statue. But not a lot of people read it.

Pulitzer's efforts still didn't bring in enough funds. By 1885, he had decided to take a different tack. He took the cause directly to the little people. Every day Pulitzer printed letters from people who could not really afford to donate money but had anyway — five cents from an office boy, one dollar from an old woman. There is some question that all the letters were actually written by these people (some of them may have been faked), but they served the purpose. Anyone reading those letters would feel downright stingy if he or she had not contributed. Altogether, some 120,000 people sent in money, and many of the contributions were in amounts of one dollar or less.

Meanwhile, Bartholdi had got his friend, Gustave Eiffel, to construct a huge iron and steel skeleton on which the hammered copper pieces would be hung. The French engineer and bridge-builder would soon become world-famous for his giant Eiffel Tower in Paris. Then Bartholdi transported the huge skeleton and the giant copper sections of his statue across the Atlantic on the ship *Isere*. But he could not put them in place until the pedestal was finished.

Work proceeded as quickly as possible on the sixty-five foot base and the eighty-nine foot pedestal. At last, in the spring of 1886, workmen began to hoist the pieces of the iron framework into place. Some of them had been mislabeled back in Paris, and that caused more delays. Then workers covered the skeleton with the copper sections, using 300,000 copper rivets to bolt the sections to each other and to the skeleton. The last rivet was driven into place on October 23, 1886. The 151-foot Liberty towered 300 feet above the harbor.

Five days later, President Grover Cleveland officially dedicated the statue. A proud but very tired Frédéric Auguste Bartholdi was there to see his dream come true. It had taken him fifteen years to do it. Sadly, his friend Édouard de Laboulaye was not there; he had died three years earlier. French and American dignitaries made speeches. Distinguished guests clapped after the speeches, which were mostly about the friendship between France and America.

The dignitaries and distinguished guests did not spend much time talking about liberty and freedom, the ideas for which the Lady stood. Even the official poem written for the occasion by John Greenleaf Whittier, began, "O France, the beautiful! to thee/ Once more we a debt of love we owe." Only one newspaper, the *New York Herald*, mentioned that as the ceremony took place a steamship crowded with European immigrants passed by.

Over the next few years, it was such immigrants who gave real meaning to Miss Liberty. She became

Liberty Enlightening the World was dedicated October 28, 1886.

famous as the first thing they saw as they entered New York Harbor, standing tall, holding her torch high to light their way to freedom. By 1903, twenty years after Emma Lazarus had written the poem "The New Colossus," the poem and the statue had come to have one meaning. That year a bronze plaque engraved with the poem was permanently mounted on the pedestal of the statue.

In 1924, President Calvin Coolidge proclaimed the Statue of Liberty a National Monument. In 1956, the name of the island was finally changed from Bedloe's to Liberty Island.

In the years since the final rivet was driven into place, Lady Liberty's 2½-foot eyes in her 10-foot face have watched the United States go through many political storms. There have been times, especially during periods of war, when the nation has closed its gates to newcomers, and when it has denied liberty to some of its own citizens. Progress in technology saw the end of the steamship era, and the immigration station at Ellis Island in New York Harbor was closed.

Political and economic upheaval in the rest of the world has seen a change in the complexion of the immigrants who seek freedom in America. When Liberty first rose above the harbor, she held her lighted torch of freedom out for European immigrants. Now, they are more likely to arrive from Southeast Asia, Central and Latin America, the Caribbean, India, and Russia. These latest immigrants are also more likely to see Lady Liberty from the air. But she still has the same meaning for them as she had for the steamship-bound immigrants from Europe. Her torch shines for them, too.

The Statue of Liberty is so closely associated with the welcoming of immigrants to America that in 1972 the American Museum of Immigration opened in her base. The ideas she symbolizes have been able to weather the storms of international war and national unrest. Her creator wanted to honor the United States for surviving one hundred years as a free, democratic society. By the time she was one hundred years old, that free and democratic society had celebrated its two hundredth anniversary. And no one could imagine a United States of America *without* its Statue of Liberty.

The Lady
Gets a Facelift

4

While the ideas she symbolizes are as healthy and strong as they were a century ago, the Statue of Liberty herself was not as lucky. The work that Bartholdi and Eiffel did in the 1880s was the best that could be done at the time, and the materials and techniques they used were the most modern. But a century of harsh Atlantic storms, salt water and salt-filled air, combined with man-made enemies like acid rain and pollution, did great damage to the statue.

Her once-gleaming copper skin, long since turned green from natural weathering, was full of thousands of holes where copper rivets had popped out. Her iron framework had weakened, and parts of it had bent and changed shape after decades of stress. Originally, there were asbestos pads between the iron armatures and the copper skin. These prevented contact between the two metals. But the pads crumbled away, and the copper corroded the iron. The torch and the arm were originally designed so that people could climb up into them. But as early as 1916 they were judged unsafe and closed to the public.

The inside of Liberty's head shows not only the lights behind the windows of her crown, but the graffiti left by millions of visitors.

Although it meant well, the public had also proved itself to be unsafe for the Statue of Liberty. The National Parks Service, which cares for both the statue and Ellis Island, estimates that in the years leading up to 1985, when Liberty Island was closed to the public so the statue could be refurbished, some 2,500 people a day visited the statue, climbing up its 168 steps or riding up the elevator that was installed in 1931. All those people represented a lot of tramping feet and groping hands . . . and loving lips! (In 1947 the inside of the statue got a coat of lipstick-proof paint.) Over the years, especially during the 1970s, many different groups chose the Statue of Liberty as the place to make known their beliefs that they were *not* enjoying the liberties that she symbolized. Among others, these groups included American Indians and Puerto Rican nationalists. Old Lady Liberty withstood it all, but just barely.

On May 18, 1982, President Ronald Reagan announced the formation of the Statue of Liberty-Ellis Island Centennial Commission to raise money to restore both the Statue of Liberty and Ellis Island in time for the celebration of Lady Liberty's one hundredth birthday. The Commission, which was headed by Lee Iacocca, the chairman of the board of the Chrysler Corporation, was charged with raising the money needed not just to restore the statue and the old immigration station but also to make them more accessible to handicapped people. The goal was $230 million.

While that is a lot of money, the Statue of Liberty-Ellis Island Commission had a much easier time waging its campaign than the committee that had raised the money for the statue's base and pedestal a century earlier. In the 1980s, there was no question about what the Statue of Liberty stood for or how much she meant to Americans and non-Americans. She may be just a statue, but she has become exactly the symbol of freedom that Frédéric Auguste Bartholdi wanted her to be. For Americans, letting her fall apart would have been like burning the Constitution! And so, they raised the money.

There was one way that the 1980s fundraising campaign was like the one back in the 1880s. A great deal of the $230 million came in small contributions from ordinary people. Many, many small sums of money came from people who had arrived in America as immigrants. They remembered how their first sight of the Statue of Liberty had filled their hearts with joy and hope. Just as the Lady has become a symbol of what America has given, so giving money to restore her was a way to give something back to America.

The United States is not a perfect country. It does not offer equal freedom or opportunities to all its people. But the Statue of Liberty stands tall above the everyday affairs of men and women. She

Repair scaffolding around the torch. The torch was later taken down and rebuilt separately.

stands for what *can* be. The Americans who helped to restore her have put their faith in the idea that what can be, will be, some day. Because of them, when that day comes, Lady Liberty's torch of freedom will be shining brightly.

Lady Liberty standing tall in New York Harbor.

A closeup of Liberty's head under repair.

Vital Statistics of the Statue

Height from base of foundation to torch	305 ft. 1 in.
Steps in Statue from base to torch	171 steps
Height from heel to head	111 ft. 1 in.
Height of torch	21 ft.
Length of hand	16 ft. 5 in.
Length of index finger	8 ft.
Size of fingernail	13 in. x 10 in.
Length of face, chin to cranium	17 ft. 3 in.
Width of eye	2 ft. 6 in.
Length of nose	4 ft. 6 in.
Width of mouth	3 ft.
Number of windows in crown	25 windows
Number of rays in diadem (representing the seven seas and seven continents)	7
Weight of copper used in Statue	100 tons
Weight of steel used in Statue	125 tons

Plan of Repairs

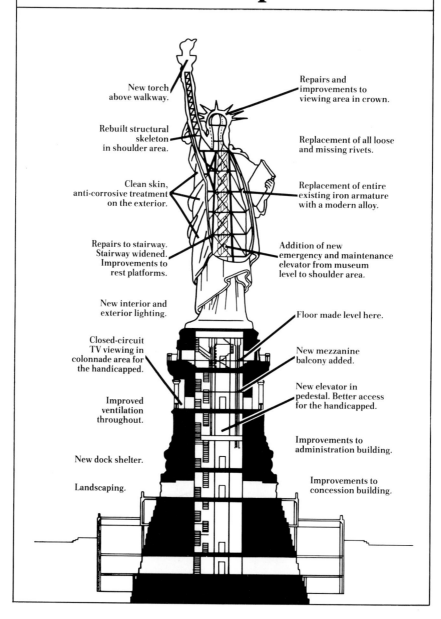

New torch above walkway.

Repairs and improvements to viewing area in crown.

Rebuilt structural skeleton in shoulder area.

Replacement of all loose and missing rivets.

Clean skin, anti-corrosive treatment on the exterior.

Replacement of entire existing iron armature with a modern alloy.

Repairs to stairway. Stairway widened. Improvements to rest platforms.

Addition of new emergency and maintenance elevator from museum level to shoulder area.

New interior and exterior lighting.

Floor made level here.

Closed-circuit TV viewing in colonnade area for the handicapped.

New mezzanine balcony added.

New elevator in pedestal. Better access for the handicapped.

Improved ventilation throughout.

Improvements to administration building.

New dock shelter.

Landscaping.

Improvements to concession building.

The Statue of Liberty

Index

46

Photo credits:

Photos courtesy of Circle Line Sightseeing Yachts, p. 8; Bartholdi Museum, Colmar, p. 19; Museum of the City of New York, p. 20; Rare Books Division, New York Public Library, Astor, Lenox & Tilden Foundations, pp. 22, 28, 29; collection of Andrew J. Spano, pp. 24, 25; Library of Congress, pp. 22, 36, 39, 42; The New-York Historical Society, p. 32; National Park Service, pp. 40, 48.